Good Eating's
BEST
OF THE BEST

Great recipes of the past decade
from the Chicago Tribune test kitchen

Edited by Carol Mighton Haddix

S
SURREY
BOOKS

**An Agate Imprint
Chicago**

Printed in the United States

10 9 8 7 6 5 4 3 2 1

Surrey Books is an imprint of Agate Publishing. Agate books are available in bulk at discount prices.
For more information, go to agatepublishing.com.

Table of Contents

Acknowledgements

Thanks are due to many people — staffers in the past and in the present — who made the Chicago Tribune Good Eating section a reality for the last 10 years and to those who helped make this book possible:

Editors/management
Linda Bergstrom
Gerould Kern
Sean McClure
Colin McMahon
Elaine Varvatos
Randall Weissman
Joycelyn Winnecke

Staff writers/editors
Bill Daley
Renee Enna
Joe Gray
Judy Hevrdejs
Robin Mather Jenkins
Tracy Maple
Emily Nunn
William Rice

Freelance columnists
JeanMarie Brownson
James P. DeWan

Book designers
Chuck Burke
Nicole Dudka

Section art director
Catherine Nichols

Photographers
John Dziekan
Bob Fila
Bill Hogan
Bonnie Trafelet

Photo editors
Itasca Wiggins
Michael Zajakowski

Publisher
Doug Seibold

Test kitchen directors
Donna Pierce
Raeanne Sarazen

Testers and food stylists
Mark Graham
Corrine Kozlak
Joan Moravek
Lisa Schumacher

Introduction

SO MANY RECIPES! Some days in the Tribune test kitchen, we're testing and tasting multiple versions of cookies, cakes or casseroles. By the end of such days, we're groaning. And, at the end of each year as we scroll through all the recipes in the Good Eating section of the Chicago Tribune, the thought of all the calories we consumed really hits home.

Ah, I know what you're saying: "Quit griping! You guys have the best jobs around."

OK, it's true. We chowed down on a lot of great food in the past 10 years. We tasted our way through thousands of recipes from Chicago, the rural Midwest, the nation and the world. We brought back recipes from Golconda, Ill., and Kerala, India. We sampled the gourmet sauces of famous chefs and the homey favorites of teenage cooks. We collected recipes from cooking teachers, authors, farmers and Tribune writers and editors.

The recipes and stories in Good Eating over the decade reflected what was happening in the food world. We looked at the benefits of a return to slow cooking in contrast to our fast-food lifestyles but also at how to make salad dressing in a flash. We visited with an Illinois cheesemaker who turns her goats' milk into ethereal cheeses. And we championed more ethnic cooking from places such as Vietnam, Japan and Argentina. We reported on the movement toward buying local,

sustainable produce in urban farmers markets. We urged readers to take up stir-frying as a quick, healthful cooking method and shared ingredients for the perfect North African chermoula spice mix.

The variety of recipes was amazing, from the rich and satisfying macaroni and cheese developed by former test kitchen chef Mark Graham to the surprising grilled meatloaf from Weber Grill restaurant. One favorite dip combined chopped bacon, lettuce and tomato for a new take on a BLT — and it didn't last long at our tasting. In the last 10 years, we saw a yearning from readers for these kinds of comfort dishes.

Since 2000, we also gave thumbs up to many grilled foods, from slow-smoked meats and seared vegetables, to the robust salads made with them. We tested new or unusual ingredients and fell in love with them: Meyer lemons, spicy chipotle chilies and Marcona almonds from Spain. We watched the low-carbohydrate diet trend morph into the no-gluten diet trend. And we saw the continued popularity of protein foods, from the resurrected egg to the rise of sustainably raised pork, beef, lamb and chicken.

Toward the end of the decade, pork reigned. When we looked back at the stories in Good Eating, the succulent, flavorful meat popped up again and again in different guises: a little bacon flavoring a squash risotto, a shoulder braised in whiskey, a homemade pork sausage flavored with maple.

Spicy dishes grew in popularity as Americans searched for more flavor in their food. We followed the exciting exploration of ethnic cuisines as ingredients became more and more available to cooks. Italian still dominates, but Southeast Asian, Spanish and Latin cuisines are coming on fast.

Quick-cooking dishes were many of our favorites, reflecting today's emphasis on easy-to-make recipes that still carry loads of flavor. They often originated in our Fast Food column (formerly called Dinner Tonight!), which has generated plenty of recipes that can be prepared in 30 minutes or less.

We saw more vegetarian recipes (lots of risotto and pasta and more whole grains) and more "raw" dishes, a growing trend reflected in cookbooks and restaurants.

And we eagerly awaited those special-occasion desserts! Our favorites included the rich butterscotch praline ice cream sundae from the Atwood Café, a tangy lemon meringue tart from freelance writer Matt McMillen and an amusing, after-Halloween pots de crème made with chocolate peanut butter cups.

OUR KITCHEN: All of those dishes went through testing and tasting in our test kitchen. The Chicago Tribune is one of the few newspapers in this country with a working test kitchen. Ours is located near the newsroom on the fourth floor of Tribune Tower. It's not large, but it suits our mission just fine: to provide recipes that are reliable, accurate and lead to successful dishes for readers.

The latest version of the kitchen, which dates to 1995, is a clean, modern space with enough room for two test cooks to work side by side. Its dark granite counters and light gray cupboards still look up to date. The room is warmed by the rows of cookbooks on shelves above the cabinets on one side of the room and the maple butcher-block desk on another.

It's not surprising that the kitchen draws staffers who often can smell the aromas of sauteed onions or baked cookies. When it's time to rate recipes, volunteers are not hard to find.

The test kitchen is where we fine-tune the ingredients, measurements and steps so that each recipe is the best possible. The test cooks rate each recipe on ease of preparation, and food editors and writers score the completed dish on appearance, texture and flavor. The rating sheets are used to determine if each recipe is good enough to appear in the paper. The question we often ask: "Is this a recipe I would make at home?" If the answer is yes, it appears in the section. Once edited, recipes are sent to dietitian Jodie Shield for nutritional analysis, an extra

benefit for readers who may be watching calories or fat or other nutrients.

Many of the prepared dishes are photographed in the photo studio located through the back door of the kitchen—certainly a convenient location for those times when a souffle is just hot from the oven, or bowls of ice cream are ready and waiting in the kitchen freezer for their time in the spotlight.

The recipes in this book began in that kitchen and were selected by staff members as our "best" recipes. At each year's end, we chose those that rated a "yum" or "I-would-make-this-at-home" vote, then printed the top 10 or 12 in Good Eating. For this book, we combed through them to pick the "best of the best." These are the recipes that stood out for us, ones that delivered exciting aromas, textures and flavors.

Although it has been 10 years of change in the kitchen, much remains the same. Flavorful dishes remain our goal, week in and week out. We hope you enjoy this culinary travel guide through the past decade. And if you have your own Tribune favorite recipes not included here, let us know. Maybe our next cookbook will feature your selections. Email us at foods@tribune.com and put "reader favorites" in the subject line.

—*Carol Mighton Haddix, Food Editor*

1
Starters

BLT dip

Prep: 15 minutes   **Cooking:** 6 minutes   **Makes:** 3 cups

This recipe for a June 2008 cover story on classic party dips was developed by former test kitchen director Donna Pierce. Serve with pita crisps, kettle chips or toast points brushed with olive oil.

4 slices bacon
3 green onions, thinly sliced
1/4 cup each: mayonnaise, low-fat Greek yogurt
1/4 cup arugula, chopped
1/4 teaspoon salt
Freshly ground pepper
1 pint grape tomatoes, quartered

1 Place the bacon in a medium skillet over medium heat; cook, turning, until crisp, about 6 minutes. Transfer to a paper towel-slined plate.

2 Combine the onions, mayonnaise, yogurt, arugula, salt and pepper to taste in a food processor; pulse until chunky, about 5 times. Transfer to a medium bowl.

3 Crumble the bacon into the bowl; stir into the mayonnaise mixture. Stir in the tomatoes.

Nutrition information
Per 1 tablespoon serving: 13 calories, 1 g fat, 0 g saturated fat, 1 mg cholesterol, 0 g carbohydrates, 0 g protein, 32 mg sodium, 0 g fiber

Editor's Tip: As with most simple recipes, the quality of your ingredients can be important. For this dip, choose bacon with robust flavor, such as an apple-wood smoked version. Look for artisanal bacons at specialty markets. If it is tomato season, feel free to substitute the grape tomatoes with any locally grown, diced tomatoes.

Mas bean dip

Prep: 15 minutes **Cooking:** 1 hour, 20 minutes **Makes:** 3 cups, 12 servings

A reader in 2001 requested this delicious white bean dip from the now-closed Mas restaurant in Chicago. After we tracked down the recipe and tried it, we were glad she asked for it!

1 cup dried white beans, such as great Northern or cannellini
1/4 pound slab bacon or 4 slices thick-cut bacon, diced
1 clove garlic, crushed
2 sprigs fresh thyme
1 tablespoon each: ground cumin, chili powder
1 tablespoon minced canned chipotle chili in adobo sauce
1 teaspoon salt, plus more to taste
3/4 cup olive oil
Freshly ground pepper

1 Wash beans in colander, discarding any discolored or shriveled ones; set aside. Cook bacon in large pot over medium-low heat until bacon is cooked, but not crisp. Add garlic; cook 1 minute. Add beans, thyme and enough water to cover by at least 3 inches. Heat to a boil. Reduce heat; partly cover. Simmer, skimming foam that rises, until tender, about 1 hour, 20 minutes.

2 Drain beans. Remove thyme stalks. Transfer bean mixture to a blender. Add cumin, chili powder, chipotle and 1 teaspoon of the salt to blender. Blend to mix. Slowly add olive oil; blend until desired consistency is reached. Season to taste with salt and pepper.

Nutrition information
Per 1/4 cup: 190 calories, 15 g fat, 2 g saturated fat,
3 mg cholesterol, 285 mg sodium, 4 g protein,
9 g carbohydrates, 3 g fiber

Editor's Tip: Dried beans can swell to two or three times their volume after soaking and cooking. If you would like to save time by using canned beans in this recipe, drain and rinse them well. You'll need about 3 cups (or two 15-ounce cans).

Butternut squash soup

Prep: 30 minutes **Cooking:** 50 minutes **Makes:** 8 servings

Personal chef Cali Bergold shared this rich squash soup with the Tribune in 2005. She often garnishes it with a drizzle of basil leaves blended with olive oil. Look for garam masala in spice stores, Indian markets and some supermarkets.

1 medium butternut squash, halved lengthwise, seeds removed
3 tablespoons unsalted butter
3 yellow onions, chopped
3 cans (14 ½ ounces each) chicken broth
1 tablespoon plus 1 ½ teaspoons toasted garam masala or curry powder, see note
1 tablespoon honey
1/4 teaspoon freshly grated nutmeg
1 cup whipping cream or milk
3 tablespoons dry sherry
1/4 teaspoon coarse salt
Freshly ground pepper

1 Heat oven to 375 degrees. Place squash flesh-side down on greased baking sheet. Bake until knife-tender, 40-45 minutes. Scoop out the flesh; set aside.

2 Meanwhile, melt butter in a large skillet over medium heat; cook onions until very soft but not brown, about 10 minutes.

3 Puree onions and squash in a food processor in batches; transfer to a large saucepan. Whisk in broth, garam masala, honey and nutmeg. Heat to a simmer over medium heat. Cook, stirring often, 10 minutes. Stir in the cream, sherry, salt and pepper to taste. Serve hot.

Note
Toast garam masala in a dry skillet over high heat, stirring, until fragrant, about 1 minute.

Nutrition information
Per serving: 238 calories, 16 g fat, 10 g saturated fat, 52 mg cholesterol, 20 g carbohydrates, 5 g protein, 581 mg sodium, 4 g fiber

Spiced organic carrot soup

Prep: 30 minutes **Cooking:** 40 minutes **Makes:** 4 servings

For the fall installment of our 2006 "Season by Season" series, writer Bill Daley asked chef Bruce Sherman of Chicago's North Pond restaurant for his unique soup flavored with ginger and coriander.

1 tablespoon olive oil
1 shallot, thinly sliced
1 clove garlic, chopped
1 piece (1/2-inch long) ginger root, chopped
1/2 rib celery, thinly sliced
1 pound organic carrots, thinly sliced
1 head fennel, white bulb only, cored, thinly sliced
1/2 teaspoon each: salt, freshly ground pepper, ground coriander
2 cans (14 ½ ounces each) chicken broth
1/2 stick (1/4 cup) butter, cubed

1 Heat the oil in a heavy, medium saucepan over medium-high heat; add shallot, garlic, ginger and celery. Cook, stirring, until slightly softened but not browned, about 2 minutes. Stir in the carrots, fennel, salt and pepper. Cook until the carrots and fennel begin to soften but do not brown, about 6 minutes.

2 Stir in the coriander; cook, stirring, 1 minute. Stir in the chicken broth. Heat to a boil; reduce heat to a simmer. Cook until the carrots and fennel pieces can be easily mashed, about 25 minutes.

3 Puree the vegetable mixture in a blender or food processor. Pulse in pieces of butter, one at a time, until very smooth, about 2 minutes. Strain the mixture through a fine-meshed strainer into the saucepan; heat over medium heat, about 3 minutes.

Nutrition information
Per serving: 239 calories, 16 g fat, 8 g saturated fat, 30 mg cholesterol, 18 g carbohydrates, 7 g protein, 1,121 mg sodium, 5 g fiber

Cherry tomato and walnut pizza

Prep: 15 minutes **Cooking:** 10 minutes **Makes:** 8 appetizer servings

Using a prebaked pizza crust makes for quick appetizers for a party. We topped one of the crusts with cherry tomatoes and walnuts for a 2009 Fast Food column.

- 1 tablespoon vegetable or olive oil
- 1 (12-inch) unseasoned prebaked pizza crust
- 2 cups (about half of a 5-ounce bag) baby spinach
- 1 pint cherry tomatoes, halved
- 3/4 cup chopped walnuts
- 1 ½ teaspoons herbes de Provence
- 1/2 teaspoon salt
- Freshly ground black pepper
- 1 package (8 ounces) low-fat shredded mozzarella or Italian cheese blend

1 Heat the oven to 400 degrees or according to crust directions. Brush the oil on the pizza crust. Scatter the spinach on the crust. Distribute the halved tomatoes over. Sprinkle the nuts over the pizza. Season with the dried herb mix, salt and pepper to taste. Top with cheese.

2 Bake according to crust directions, 10-12 minutes. Remove from oven; let cool 5 minutes before slicing.

Nutrition information
Per serving: 667 calories, 39 g fat, 8 g saturated fat, 30 mg cholesterol, 51 g carbohydrates, 34 g protein, 997 mg sodium, 5 g fiber

Editor's Tip: This topping also works well on English muffins; try them for after-school snacks. With a simple switch of seasonings, you also can change the flavor. Use Italian herbs such as basil, rosemary or sage. Or give it a Mexican twist with a mix of cumin, oregano and chili powder.

Artichoke and pesto pizza

Prep: 15 minutes **Cooking:** 7 minutes **Makes:** 4 appetizer servings

While hankering for a New Haven pizza, writer Bill Daley came up with this combo of pesto, artichoke and toasted pine nuts, based on the "Pete's A Pie" pizza served at Randy's Wooster Street Pizza, a small chain of shops in Connecticut. It appeared in a 2005 Dinner Tonight column

1/4 cup bottled or fresh pesto sauce
1 pre-baked pizza crust (9-inch) or dough round
1 jar (6 ounces) marinated artichoke hearts, drained
1/4 cup toasted pine nuts, see note
1 cup shredded mozzarella cheese

1 Heat oven to 450 degrees. Spread pesto thinly over pizza crust. Distribute the drained artichoke hearts evenly over the pie; sprinkle with the pine nuts. Cover with mozzarella cheese.

2 Bake until the crust bottom is golden and crisp and the cheese has melted, 7-10 minutes. Slice into wedges.

Note
To toast pine nuts, place in a small, heavy skillet over medium heat; cook, stirring often, until the nuts are browned, about 5 minutes.

Nutrition information
Per serving: 281 calories, 18 g fat, 6 g saturated fat, 20 mg cholesterol, 16 g carbohydrates, 14 g protein, 371 mg sodium, 4 g fiber

White and black martini (a.k.a. Soxtini)

Prep: 5 minutes **Makes:** 1 drink

"Beer, brats and baseball are the Holy Trinity for Chicago sports fans," wrote food writer Bill Daley in an October 2005 article. "But let's face it, when a hometown team is in the World Series you gotta 'Sox' it up, party-wise. Our suggestion: Put this triple martini threat into your entertaining playbook."

  4 ounces vodka
  1/2 ounce gin
  Pearl onion, black olive

Shake the vodka and gin in a cocktail shaker stocked with ice until almost frosty. Strain into a martini glass, garnish with a pearl onion and black olive.

2
Meats

Home-style BBQ meatloaf

Prep: 20 minutes   **Cooking:** 2 hours   **Cook:** 55 minutes   **Makes:** 6 servings

This unusual but delicious grilled meatloaf is adapted from a recipe from Weber Grill restaurants. It calls for two kinds of bottled barbecue sauce, one for the meat mixture and one for basting. We included the recipe in a 4th of July story in 2002 about grilling inexpensive meats.

1 tablespoon vegetable oil
1 Spanish onion, peeled, chopped
2 pounds ground beef, 80 percent lean preferred
1/2 cup dry bread crumbs, such as Japanese panko
1/3 cup bottled barbecue sauce
2 large eggs
3 tablespoons ketchup
1 tablespoon steak sauce
2 teaspoons salt
1 ½ tablespoons hickory smoke barbecue sauce

1 Heat oven to 325 degrees. Heat oil in a heavy skillet; add onion. Cook over medium heat until onion softens and begins to caramelize, about 10 minutes.

2 Transfer onion to large bowl. Add beef, bread crumbs, 1/3 cup barbecue sauce, eggs, ketchup, steak sauce and salt. Mix ingredients until thoroughly blended. Pack into an 8-by-4-inch loaf pan. Smooth the top; brush with a thin layer of the hickory smoke barbecue sauce.

3 Place loaf in a baking pan to catch any overflow; cook in oven until center reaches 155 degrees on instant-read meat thermometer, about 40 minutes. Remove from oven; let cool. Refrigerate at least 2 hours or overnight.

4 Prepare a grill for indirect, medium heat. Remove loaf from pan; slice crosswise into 6 equal slices. Place slices directly over coals; grill 2-3 minutes. Turn; grill 2 minutes. Move slices to cooler part of grill; brush lightly with hickory-flavored sauce. Grill 2-3 minutes to glaze.

Nutrition information
Per serving: 375 calories, 23 g fat, 8 g saturated fat, 160 mg cholesterol, 1,200 mg sodium, 13 g carbohydrate, 26 g protein, 1 g fiber

Double wasabi brisket

Prep: 30 minutes   **Marinate/rest:** 9 hours   **Cook:** 5 hours, 45 minutes   **Makes:** 12 servings

An Asian take on barbecued brisket, this recipe was developed in the test kitchen and accompanied a 2004 story about wasabi. The brisket can be cooked a day ahead, then finished with the sauce an hour before serving. Wasabi powder and paste are sold in Asian and spice markets, and some larger supermarkets.

Rub and brisket:
2 cloves garlic, finely chopped
1 piece (3 inches long) ginger root, finely chopped
3 tablespoons light brown sugar
2 tablespoons each: Chinese five-spice powder, ground cumin, sweet paprika
1 tablespoon each: wasabi powder, black pepper
2 ½ teaspoons coarse salt
1 teaspoon each: ground cardamom, ground coriander
1 beef brisket, first cut, trimmed, about 4 pounds

Finishing sauce:
2 cloves garlic, finely chopped
1/2 cup soy sauce
3 tablespoons each: Thai sweet red chili sauce, wasabi paste, brown sugar
1 tablespoon Dijon mustard
1/2 teaspoon salt
Freshly ground pepper

1 Combine rub ingredients in a small bowl; set aside. Place brisket in a 13-by-9-inch pan lined with foil overlapping by 7 inches on each side to allow the brisket to be sealed in the foil. Press spice rub into all sides of brisket; arrange brisket fat side up in the pan. Seal; refrigerate at least 8 hours.

2 Remove brisket from refrigerator; set aside at room temperature 30 minutes. Heat oven to 350 degrees. Cook brisket in oven 1 hour. Reduce heat to 275 degrees; bake until tender, 4-4 1/2 hours. Remove from oven; let stand 20 minutes.

3 Meanwhile, for sauce, whisk together all ingredients in a small bowl; set aside. Partially slice the brisket in thin slices against the grain, cutting almost through the meat but leaving the bottom attached. Pour sauce over brisket. Reseal foil package; return to oven. Cook until fork tender, 45 minutes-1 hour.

Nutrition information
Per serving: 299 calories, 13 g fat, 4 g saturated fat, 89 mg cholesterol, 14 g carbohydrates, 30 g protein, 1,553 mg sodium, 1 g fiber

Grilled pork tenderloin with chimichurri

Prep: 20 minutes **Marinate:** 2 hours **Cook:** 34 minutes **Makes:** 4 servings

This recipe was included in a Memorial Day cover story in 2005, "Hot Grills, Cool Wines." Chimichurri is an Argentine herb sauce served with beef, chicken and pork. The suggested wine pairings were both Chilean: an Aresti Gewurztraminer or a Veranda Pinot Noir.

3 cloves garlic
1 cup packed flat-leaf parsley sprigs
1/2 cup extra-virgin olive oil
1/4 cup each: fresh oregano leaves, packed cilantro sprigs
1 teaspoon each: ground cumin, crushed red pepper
1/2 teaspoon salt
Juice of 1 large lemon
2 pork tenderloins, about 1 pound each

1 Combine garlic, parsley, olive oil, oregano, cilantro, cumin, red pepper, salt and lemon juice in a food processor or blender; process until pureed.

2 Refrigerate 1/2 cup of the sauce in a bowl for serving. Place pork tenderloins in a large food storage bag; pour remaining sauce over pork. Refrigerate 2-12 hours, turning occasionally.

3 Prepare grill for medium heat. Remove pork from marinade, wiping marinade off pieces. Grill pork, turning often, until cooked to 160 degrees, 15-25 minutes, moving pork to cooler parts of the grill to avoid burning. Let stand 5 minutes. Slice pork; serve with the reserved sauce.

Nutrition information
Per serving: 456 calories, 28 g fat, 5 g saturated fat, 126 mg cholesterol, 3 g carbohydrates, 46 g protein, 316 mg sodium, 1 g fiber

Asian braised pork with cocoa

Prep: 15 minutes   **Cook:** 3 hours, 45 minutes   **Makes:** 8 servings

The late chef Paul Wildermuth contributed this recipe for a story on chefs' surprise ingredients. The slow-cooked pork has a touch of cocoa as a flavoring agent. Serve the pork with steamed rice or Asian noodles, or spooned into lettuce cups. Star anise is an element of Chinese five-spice powder. Look for it whole in Asian aisles of the supermarket or in Chinese food markets.

1 pork shoulder roast, about 4 ½ pounds
2 teaspoons salt
Freshly ground pepper
2 tablespoons peanut oil
6 cans (14 ½ ounces each) chicken broth
3 green onions, thinly sliced
3 cloves garlic, minced
3 whole star anise
2 dried arbol or other hot chilies
1 piece (2 inches long) ginger root, peeled, thinly sliced
1/2 white onion, thinly sliced
1/2 cup each: brown sugar, soy sauce
1/2 teaspoon whole black peppercorns
1/2 cup plum or rice wine
1/4 cup cornstarch
2 teaspoons Dutch-process cocoa powder

1 Season the pork with the salt and freshly ground pepper to taste. Heat the oil over high heat in a large Dutch oven; sear the meat on all sides until well-browned, about 3 minutes per side. Add the broth, green onions, garlic, star anise, chilies, ginger root, white onion, brown sugar, soy sauce and peppercorns. Heat to boiling; reduce heat to simmer. Cover; cook until fork tender, about 3 hours.

2 Remove meat from liquid; set aside on a platter. Increase heat to high; boil liquid uncovered until reduced by one-fourth, about 20 minutes. Strain liquid; return liquid to Dutch oven. Combine plum wine, corn-starch and cocoa powder in a small bowl. Whisk into liquid. Heat to a boil; cook, stirring, until thick, about 2 minutes. Shred meat with a fork or hands; return meat to sauce. Cook until heated through, about 1 minute.

Nutrition information
Per serving: 450 calories, 21 g fat, 7 g saturated fat, 120 mg cholesterol, 2655 mg sodium, 20 g carbohydrate, 42 g protein, 1 g fiber

Maple-sage breakfast sausage

Prep: 25 minutes   **Chill:** 10 minutes   **Cook:** 10 minutes   **Makes:** 8 servings

For a 2007 "Slow Cooking" column, former staff writer Robin Mather Jenkins wrote: "Homemade sausage takes less time than you think and delivers stellar results."

1 ½ pounds pork shoulder, lean and fat,
　cut into 1/2-inch cubes
1/4 cup cold water
2 tablespoons pure maple syrup
1 ½ teaspoons each: salt, minced fresh sage
1 teaspoon each: freshly ground pepper,
　hot red pepper sauce
1/2 teaspoon grated nutmeg

1 Place the cubed pork on a plate; freeze 10 minutes to firm. Transfer in batches to bowl of food processor; pulse until pork is coarsely chopped in pea-size pieces. Transfer pork to a large bowl; add remaining ingredients. Using hands, combine ingredients until well blended. Refrigerate until needed, up to 3 days.

2 Shape into 16 equal-size patties about 1/2-inch thick. Heat a large, heavy skillet over medium heat. Cook patties, in batches, until well browned, about 5 minutes; turn. Cook 5 minutes. Transfer to a paper towel-lined plate.

Nutrition information
Per serving: 138 calories, 6 g fat, 2 g saturated fat, 50 mg cholesterol, 4 g carbohydrates, 17 g protein, 486 mg sodium, 0 g fiber

Editor's Tip: If you are adventurous enough to make your own sausage patties, then you'll want to make your pancakes from scratch too. It's easy: Whisk together in a large bowl 2 cups flour, 2 teaspoons sugar, 1 teaspoon each baking soda and salt. Whisk together in a large measuring cup 2 large eggs, 2 cups buttermilk and 1/4 cup melted butter or vegetable oil. Pour into flour mixture; whisk lightly just to moisten the flour. Spoon onto very lightly oiled hot griddle to make 3-inch pancakes. Cook until bubbles form on top, about 2 minutes; turn. Cook until lightly browned, about 2 minutes. Makes about 20 pancakes.

Pork chops with figs and walnuts

Prep: 15 minutes   **Cook:** 30 minutes   **Makes:** 4 servings

Former staff writer Robin Mather Jenkins jazzed up a baked pork chop with this great stuffing of figs and nuts for a Dinner Tonight column in 2007. The fig and walnut stuffing also would work well with chicken breasts.

4 boneless pork loin chops
1 package (9 ounces) dried mission figs
1 small onion, quartered
1 clove garlic
2 slices whole-grain bread, torn into small pieces
1/4 cup chopped walnuts
2 tablespoons fig or raspberry jam
1/2 teaspoon each: dried thyme, salt
Freshly ground pepper

1 Heat oven to 375 degrees. Make a horizontal cut about halfway through each pork chop to form a pocket, but do not cut through the chops; set aside.

2 Combine figs, onion and garlic in a food processor or blender; pulse several times, until mixture is just coarsely chopped. Transfer mixture to a medium bowl. Stir in bread, walnuts, jam, thyme and salt; season with pepper to taste. Divide mixture among the 4 chops, stuffing it into each pocket.

3 Place chops in shallow baking dish. (If you have more stuffing than pork, add remainder to the baking dish; lay stuffed chops over extra stuffing.) Bake until pork is no longer pink, about 30 minutes.

Nutrition information
Per serving: 579 calories, 22 g fat, 7 g saturated fat, 105 mg cholesterol, 56 g carbohydrates, 42 g protein, 435 mg sodium, 8 g fiber

Provencal veal chops with warm bell-pepper slaw

Prep: 20 minutes **Cook:** 20 minutes **Makes:** 4 servings

Veal is an expensive choice for a weeknight dinner, but if you are celebrating a special occasion, it is worth it for its mild, versatile flavor. This recipe, created by Carol Mighton Haddix for a 2004 Dinner Tonight column, includes the spice mixture known as herbes de Provence and a topping of lightly cooked bell peppers. This recipe also would work well with lamb chops.

    3 tablespoons herbes de Provence
    2 tablespoons olive oil
    1 tablespoon sherry wine vinegar or balsamic vinegar
    1/2 teaspoon salt
    1/4 teaspoon freshly ground pepper
    4 veal chops, about 1-inch thick
    3 cloves garlic, minced
    3 bell peppers, choice of red, yellow and purple, seeded, cut into thin strips

1 Mix herbs, olive oil, vinegar, salt and pepper in large bowl. Add veal chops, turning to coat all sides. Heat a large, heavy skillet over high heat; add the veal chops, reserving the marinade. Cook veal to brown one side, about 2 minutes. Turn; brown second side, 2 minutes. Turn heat to low; cook until desired doneness, about 5 minutes. Remove to a platter; keep warm.

2 Add garlic and peppers to same skillet. Turn heat to high; stir-fry until peppers are crisp-tender, about 2 minutes. Add reserved marinade; stir-fry 1 minute. Spoon peppers over veal chops.

Nutrition information
Per serving: 322 calories, 20 g fat, 7 g saturated fat, 110 mg cholesterol, 7 g carbohydrates, 28 g protein, 394 mg sodium, 0 g fiber

Editor's Tip: Many cooks avoid using veal in their menus because of concerns about how the animals are raised in small pens. But today it is easier to find natural veal products from pastured, grass-fed animals. Such meat is a deeper pink color and has a very mild beefy flavor.

3
Poultry

Kickin' chicken soup

Prep: 25 minutes   **Cook:** 15 minutes   **Makes:** 8 servings

A bowl of homemade chicken soup doesn't have to take hours to get to the table. This weeknight recipe from 2003 is hearty enough for the main course and uses a few convenience products to speed the process. Include the chili seeds for more heat.

2 large, boneless chicken breasts
3 tablespoons canola oil
1 large onion, chopped
3 cloves garlic, minced
1 jalapeno chili, minced
1 carton (32 ounces) low-sodium chicken broth
1 can (15 ½ ounces) black beans
3 cups fresh or frozen corn kernels
1 teaspoon salt or to taste
1/2 teaspoon ground red pepper or hot sauce
Juice of 1 lime
Freshly ground black pepper
1/2 cup minced cilantro
Shredded Monterey jack cheese, tortilla chips, optional

1 Heat broiler. Place chicken on a broiler pan; broil, turning once, until juices run clear, about 10 minutes. Meanwhile, heat oil in a large saucepan over medium heat. Add onion, garlic and chili; cook until soft, about 3 minutes. Add broth, beans, corn, salt, red pepper, lime juice and black pepper to taste. Heat to a boil; reduce heat to simmer.

2 Slice or shred cooked chicken; add to pan. Add cilantro. Heat through, about 1 minute. Ladle into soup bowls; top each with shredded cheese and crumbled tortilla chips, if desired.

Nutrition information
Per serving: 205 calories, 8 g fat, 1 g saturated fat, 10 mg cholesterol, 28 g carbohydrates, 10 g protein, 585 mg sodium, 6 g fiber

Panko-crusted chicken with cilantro vinaigrette

Prep: 15 minutes   **Cook:** 10 minutes   **Makes:** 4 servings

For a 2007 cover story, "Bored with the bird?", writer Bill Daley contributed this recipe using Japanese panko bread crumbs. "Panko have a coarser texture than the usual crumbs, but also a certain degree of lightness, making them an ideal coating in this dish," he wrote. Panko is available at specialty and Asian markets as well as larger supermarkets.

4 boneless, skinless chicken breast halves, flattened to 1/4-inch thickness, see note
1 teaspoon each: salt, freshly ground pepper
2 eggs, beaten
1 ½ cups panko bread crumbs
1/2 cup flour
2 tablespoons minced cilantro
3 tablespoons olive oil
Cilantro vinaigrette:
4 cloves garlic
1/2 cup chopped cilantro
Juice of 1 large lemon
1/2 cup olive oil

1 Season chicken with the salt and pepper. Place eggs, bread crumbs and flour in three separate shallow containers. Mix the cilantro into the crumbs. Heat the 3 tablespoons oil in a large skillet over medium-high heat.

2 Dip each breast in the following order to coat: flour, egg and bread crumbs. Add chicken to skillet (do not crowd). Cook until the chicken breasts are cooked through and golden brown, about 5 minutes per side; drain on paper towels.

3 Meanwhile, for the cilantro vinaigrette, place the garlic and cilantro in a blender or food processor; blend or pulse into a rough paste. Slowly add the lemon juice, blending until incorporated. Slowly drizzle in the olive oil to create an emulsion. Spoon the vinaigrette over the chicken. Refrigerate any remaining vinaigrette for another use.

Note

To flatten chicken breast halves, place them one at a time in a heavy food storage bag. Use a mallet, hammer or rolling pin to pound the chicken breast to desired thickness.

Nutrition information

Per serving: 609 calories, 31 g fat, 5 g saturated fat, 179 mg cholesterol, 43 g carbohydrates, 37 g protein, 978 mg sodium, 2 g fiber

Chicken cacciatore with red and yellow peppers

Prep: 45 minutes   **Rest:** 4 hours   **Cook:** 1 hour, 25 minutes   **Makes:** 6 servings

Freelance writer JeanMarie Brownson cooked up this savory family favorite for a 2009 Dinner at Home column. You can coat the chicken with salt the day before cooking.

1 cut-up chicken, 3 pounds
2 ½ teaspoons salt
1/4 cup olive oil
1/2 pound sliced mushrooms
1 small onion, chopped
1 large each, cored, cut into 1-inch pieces: red bell pepper, yellow bell pepper
4 cloves garlic, crushed
1 cup dry white wine
1 can (28 ounces) crushed tomatoes
1/2 cup water
2 bay leaves
1 sprig rosemary
1/4 cup minced flat leaf parsley
1/4 teaspoon freshly ground pepper

1 Season chicken with 2 teaspoons of the salt; place in bowl or storage bag. Refrigerate 4-12 hours. Heat oven to 375 degrees. Pat the chicken pieces very dry and remove excess salt. Heat the oil in a deep 12-inch (or larger) skillet over medium heat. Add the chicken, in batches if necessary, skin side down, in a single, uncrowded layer. Brown the chicken on all sides, about 10 minutes. Transfer to a large platter.

2 Add the mushrooms to the pan; cook until golden on all sides, about 5 minutes. Remove with slotted spoon to the platter. Add onion and peppers to the skillet; cook until onion is golden, about 6 minutes. Add garlic; cook 1 minute.

3 Add wine; heat to a boil, stirring to scrape up browned bits. Cook until wine reduces to almost nothing, 5 minutes. Add tomatoes, water, bay leaves, rosemary and half of the parsley. Season with 1/2 teaspoon of the salt and pepper. Return the chicken and mushrooms to the pan, nestling them into sauce.

4 Partly cover the pan; cook until the chicken juices run clear, 40 minutes. (If sauce is too thin, remove chicken and vegetables to a platter; cook the sauce over medium-high heat until desired thickness.) Sprinkle with remaining parsley.

Nutrition information

Per serving: 411 calories, 25 g fat, 6 g saturated fat, 89 mg cholesterol, 13 g carbohydrates, 32 g protein, 658 mg sodium, 3 g fiber

Chicken braised with warm spices and dried fruit

Prep: 20 minutes **Cook:** 1 hour **Makes:** 4 servings

For our 2001 series, "On the Spice Trail," the test kitchen staff developed this dish, seasoned with gentle spices and dried fruit.

2 tablespoons flour
1 teaspoon salt
Freshly ground pepper
8 chicken thighs
2 tablespoons vegetable oil
1 medium onion, diced
1/4 teaspoon each: ground cinnamon, cumin, coriander, ginger, turmeric, paprika
1/2 cup white wine
3 cups chicken broth
1/2 cup each, halved: dried apricots, dried dates
2 tablespoons unsalted butter

1 Heat oven to 350 degrees. Mix flour, salt and pepper to taste in a shallow bowl. Coat chicken lightly in flour mixture. Heat oil in large, heavy-bottomed saucepan or Dutch oven over medium-high heat. Place chicken skin-side down in batches in pan; cook until skin is golden brown and crisp, 4 minutes. Turn over; cook 4 minutes longer. Remove to a plate. Pour off all but 1 tablespoon of the oil from pan.

2 Reduce heat to medium. Add onion; cook until golden brown, about 5 minutes. Stir in cinnamon, cumin, coriander, ginger, turmeric and paprika; cook 1 minute. Add wine; cook, scraping browned bits from bottom of pan, until reduced by half, 3 minutes. Return chicken to pan. Stir in broth, dried fruit and butter; heat to a boil. Cover; braise in oven until chicken is cooked through, about 45 minutes.

Nutrition information
Per serving: 570 calories, 34 g fat, 10 g saturated fat, 130 mg cholesterol, 1,265 mg sodium, 29 g carbohydrate, 37 g protein, 3 g fiber

Duck with pear-cardamom puree and caramel almonds

Prep: 45 minutes   **Rest:** 40 minutes   **Makes:** 4 servings

Chef Andrew Zimmerman, formerly of del Toro Cafe, provided this recipe to accompany our fall installment in the 2006 "Season by Season" series. Zimmerman prefers to use Spanish marcona almonds, which have a more intense flavor and are sold at specialty stores and some supermarkets. You can substitute with blanched almonds.

Caramel almonds:
3/4 cup sugar
1/4 cup water
1 ¼ cups marcona almonds

Pear-cardamom puree:
5 cardamom seeds or 1/4 teaspoon ground cardamom
3 Bosc or other pears, peeled, cored, diced
1/4 cup water
2 tablespoons butter

Duck:
4 boneless, skin-on duck breasts, 6-8 ounces each
1/8 teaspoon each: salt, freshly ground pepper

1 For the almonds, combine the sugar and just enough of the water to moisten it in a heavy, medium saucepan over medium heat. Cook until the mixture turns golden brown and measures about 275 degrees on a candy thermometer, about 15 minutes. Stir in the almonds, stirring quickly to coat. Pour almonds onto a parchment-lined baking pan; cool. Roughly chop the almonds, removing excess caramel; set aside.

2 For the puree, heat the cardomom seeds, pears, water and butter to a simmer in a medium saucepan over medium heat; cook until the pears are tender, about 15 minutes. Puree in a blender until smooth; pass through a fine-mesh sieve. Keep warm.

3 For the duck, score the skin side of the duck in a crosshatch pattern, taking care not to cut into the flesh; season with salt and pepper. Place skin side down in a cold, dry skillet; cook the duck over medium heat until the skin has started to turn a deep golden brown, about 7 minutes. Turn; cook 3 minutes more. Transfer to a wire rack set over a plate.

4 Spoon a fourth of the pear puree onto each plate; slice each duck breast, fanning out over the puree. Scatter some of the caramelized chopped almonds over the duck.

Nutrition information
Per serving: 871 calories, 47 g fat, 10 g saturated fat, 246 mg cholesterol, 65 g carbohydrates, 52 g protein, 256 mg sodium, 8 g fiber

Pomegranate soda barbecue sauce

Prep: 10 minutes **Rest:** 25 minutes **Makes:** 1 cup

Test cook Lisa Schumacher created this sauce with pomegranate-flavored soda for a 2010 story on cooking with the new flavored sodas. Use this to glaze grilled, broiled or roasted poultry during the last 30 minutes of cooking.

  1 cup each: pomegranate soda, ketchup
  1/4 cup each: fresh lemon juice, pomegranate juice
  3 tablespoons Worcestershire sauce
  1 ½ tablespoons dark brown sugar, packed
  1 tablespoon mild molasses
  1 teaspoon grated lemon zest
  1/2 teaspoon each: garlic powder, onion powder
  1/4 teaspoon ground red pepper

Combine all ingredients in a large heavy saucepan. Heat to a boil over medium heat, stirring often. Reduce heat to medium; cook, stirring often, until thickened, about 25 minutes. Taste; adjust seasonings. Cool. Refrigerate until ready to use, up to 2 weeks.

Nutrition information
Per tablespoon: 37 calories, 0 g fat, 0 g saturated fat, 0 mg cholesterol, 10 g carbohydrates, 0 g protein, 202 mg sodium, 0 g fiber

Editor's Tip: This barbecue sauce can lend itself to many variations simply by changing the type of soda you use. Try it with a cola or ginger ale, for example. Other fruit-flavored sodas to try: orange, lemon or raspberry.

4
Seafood and Fish

Smoky tomato and seafood soup

Prep: 40 minutes   **Cook:** 40 minutes   **Makes:** 6 servings

Freelance writer JeanMarie Brownson recalled the seafood of Spain in a Dinner at Home column in 2008. She included this soup recipe that gets a smoky flavor from Spanish paprika, available in spice markets and specialty stores.

8 to 10 ripe plum tomatoes or 1 can (15 ounces) diced fire-roasted tomatoes, undrained
3 tablespoons olive oil
3 large shallots, finely chopped
1 small leek, trimmed, chopped
1 red bell pepper, seeded, chopped, or 1 bottled roasted red bell pepper, diced
6 large cloves garlic, finely chopped
1 quart vegetable broth
1 bottle (8 ounces) clam juice or water
1/2 cup dry white wine
1/4 cup tomato paste
1 teaspoon salt
3/4 teaspoon smoked sweet Spanish paprika
1 pound small fresh clams, scrubbed clean, or 1 box (16 ounces) frozen steamer clams in
   garlic butter sauce, left frozen
1/2 pound large (26-30 count) raw shrimp, peeled, deveined
1 pound boneless, skinless fish fillets, such as tilapia, pollock or snapper, cut into 1 1/2-inch pieces
1/2 pound bay scallops
Garlic mayo, optional, see recipe below
   Chopped fresh parsley and chives

1 If using fresh tomatoes, heat the broiler to high; put tomatoes on a foil-lined baking sheet. Broil 6 inches from the heat source, turning occasionally, until the skin is lightly charred on all sides, 10-12 minutes. Cool, peel and chop coarsely, collecting all the juices.

2 Heat the oil in a 4- to 5-quart Dutch oven or deep saucepan. Cook the shallots and leek until soft, about 4 minutes. Stir in the red pepper and garlic; cook 1 minute. Add the tomatoes, broth, clam juice, wine, tomato paste, salt and paprika. Simmer 15 minutes.

3 Add the clams; cook 3 minutes. Add the shrimp and fish; cook 2 minutes. Add the scallops; cook 1 minute or until all fish is opaque but still tender. Ladle the soup into wide serving bowls. Place a dollop of the garlic mayo in the center. Sprinkle with parsley and chives.

Garlic mayo: Mix 1/3 cup mayonnaise and 1 table-spoon fresh lemon juice in a small bowl. Use a garlic press to crush in 1 large clove of garlic; mix well. Add a pinch of salt if needed. This can be made up to 1 day in advance; cover and refrigerate.

Nutrition information

Per serving: 392 calories, 12 g fat, 2 g saturated fat, 211 mg cholesterol, 20 g carbohydrates, 51 g protein, 1,420 mg sodium, 3 g fiber

Salmon with orzo, oranges and olives

Prep: 20 minutes   **Cook:** 8 minutes   **Makes:** 6 servings

Salmon fillets — hearty, rich and quick to cook in the broiler — are teamed with orzo, a delicious, ricelike pasta, plus olives and oranges. The recipe appeared in a 2004 Dinner Tonight column.

2 salmon fillets, about 12 ounces each
1 teaspoon salt
Freshly ground pepper
1 cup pitted black olives, chopped
1/4 cup fresh basil, minced
2 tablespoons olive oil
1 teaspoon each: honey, orange juice
1 cup orzo, cooked according to package directions
1 orange or tangerine, peeled, seeded, divided into segments
1 tablespoon toasted sesame seeds, optional, see note

1 Heat broiler to high; place rack 6 inches from heat. Season salmon with 1/2 teaspoon of the salt and pepper to taste. Place salmon on a foil-lined broiler pan; broil until almost done, about 8 minutes. Set aside.

2 Meanwhile, mix olives, basil, oil, honey, juice, remaining 1/2 teaspoon of the salt and pepper to taste in a large bowl. Add orzo; toss to coat. Transfer to a platter. Cut salmon into pieces; place over orzo with orange segments. Sprinkle sesame seeds over all, if desired.

Note
To toast sesame seeds, place them in a dry skillet over medium-low heat. Cook, stirring, until light brown, 1-2 minutes. Watch carefully to avoid burning.

Nutrition information
Per serving: 379 calories, 16 g fat, 2 g saturated fat, 73 mg cholesterol, 28 g carbohydrates, 31 g protein, 642 mg sodium, 2 g fiber

Editor's Tip: This quick Mediterranean-style recipe can be made with other fish or seafood. Try it with tuna, red snapper or halibut. Cooking times may vary, depending on the thickness of the fillets. The general rule of thumb to cook fish through completely is 10 minutes per inch of thickness.

Walleye tacos

Prep: 25 minutes **Chill:** 30 minutes **Cook:** 10 minutes **Makes:** 6 servings

In a July 2005 cover story, "Lake Effect," former staff writer Robin Mather Jenkins wrote, "Factors from invasive species to pollution to population crashes have all but sunk commercial fishing on Lake Michigan. Scientists say the lake may never regain its pristine health and native ecosystem." She went on to describe how this situation came about and included this recipe for walleye, one of the lake's native fish.

Coleslaw:
1 bag (16 ounces) shredded cabbage and carrots
1/2 red onion, thinly sliced
1/2 cup regular or light mayonnaise
1 tablespoon cider vinegar
1 teaspoon salt
1/2 teaspoon freshly ground pepper

Fish:
2 walleye fillets, about 6 ounces each, skinned
1 teaspoon olive oil
1/2 teaspoon each: ground cumin, chipotle or regular chili powder
1/4 teaspoon each: dried oregano, salt
6 flour tortillas

1 For coleslaw, combine ingredients in a large bowl; refrigerate, covered, at least 30 minutes, stirring occasionally.

2 For fish, place fillets on a lightly greased broiler pan; brush with olive oil. Sprinkle cumin, chipotle powder, oregano and salt over fish; set aside to rest 15 minutes.

3 Heat broiler to high; place rack in center of the oven. Broil fish until lightly browned, about 10 minutes. Transfer to a bowl; flake with a fork.

4 Meanwhile, heat tortillas, in batches, in a dry skillet over medium heat until soft and puffy, about 2 minutes; turn with tongs. Cook 1 1/2 minutes. Remove to a plate; cover to keep warm. Repeat with remaining tortillas. Top each tortilla with shredded fish and coleslaw; fold tortilla over to eat.

Nutrition information
Per serving: 305 calories, 18 g fat, 3 g saturated fat, 41 mg cholesterol, 22 g carbohydrates, 12 g protein, 849 mg sodium, 3 g fiber

Lobster and grits

Prep: 25 minutes   **Cook:** 50 minutes   **Makes:** 6 servings

Tasters in the test kitchen applauded this recipe from Wilbert Jones, author of "The New Soul Food Cookbook." It appeared with a 2005 story about grits and how the coarsely ground dried corn finally is getting the recognition it deserves, thanks to the growing interest in American regional foods. Crab or shrimp can be substituted for the lobster.

4 slices smoked bacon, cut into 1/2-inch pieces
1 each, diced: onion, carrot
1/2 each, diced: red bell pepper, yellow bell pepper, green bell pepper
2 cups each, or more if needed: milk, water
1 cup quick grits (not instant)
1 cup whipping cream
1 stick (1/2 cup) unsalted butter
1 ½ cups chopped cooked lobster meat, crabmeat or shrimp
1/2 teaspoon salt
1 teaspoon white pepper
1 to 3 dashes hot red pepper sauce
2 green onions, white and some green, chopped

1 Cook the bacon in a large skillet over medium heat until brown and crisp, about 6 minutes; transfer to a paper towel to drain. Add onion, carrot and bell peppers to skillet. Cook, stirring occasionally, until vegetables soften, about 5 minutes; set aside.

2 Meanwhile, heat the milk and water to a boil in a medium, heavy saucepan over medium heat. Stir in the grits; reduce the heat to a simmer. Cook, stirring often, until mixture thickens, about 25 minutes.

3 Stir in cream and butter; cook 5 minutes. Add the lobster, salt, pepper and hot pepper sauce; cook 3 minutes. Fold in the reserved bacon and vegetables. Stir in more milk or water if the grits are too thick. Garnish with green onions.

Nutrition information
Per serving: 496 calories, 34 g fat, 20 g saturated fat, 131 mg cholesterol, 33 g carbohydrates, 16 g protein, 500 mg sodium, 2 g fiber

Shrimp hash cakes

Prep: 40 minutes   **Cook:** 45 minutes   **Makes:** 4 servings

This shrimp hash from chef Patrick O'Connell, of The Inn at Little Washington in Virginia, was included in writer Bill Daley's 2010 story about hash. O'Connell also adds lobster to this hash for a special celebration meal. The cakes can be wrapped in plastic and kept in the refrigerator for up to 12 hours before cooking.

1/2 cup shrimp or chicken stock
1/4 cup whipping cream
2 teaspoons tomato paste
1 large Yukon gold potato, peeled, diced
2 tablespoons finely chopped onion
3 tablespoons grape seed or vegetable oil
3 tablespoons diced green and red bell peppers
3 cloves garlic, minced
3/4 pound raw shrimp, peeled, deveined, chopped
1/4 cup fresh bread crumbs
2 ½ tablespoons flour
2 tablespoons chopped parsley
1/2 teaspoon grated, each: lemon zest, orange zest
1/2 teaspoon salt
Freshly ground pepper
1 egg

1 Combine the shrimp stock, cream and tomato paste in a small saucepan. Heat to a boil; reduce heat to a simmer. Cook until reduced by half. Cool the sauce to room temperature. Meanwhile, boil the potato in a saucepan of salted water to cover until just tender, about 10 minutes. Drain; set aside.

2 Cook the onions in a skillet over medium-high heat in 1 ½ tablespoons of the oil until lightly browned. Add the peppers; cook until tender. Add the garlic; cook 1 minute. Add the cooked potato; cook until lightly colored, about 10 minutes.

3 Remove the cooked vegetables to a bowl. Add shrimp, bread crumbs, flour, parsley, the lemon and orange zest. Season with salt and pepper to taste. Add the egg; fold together gently until just combined. Shape the hash into cakes about 3 inches in diameter.

4 Heat remaining 1 1/2 tablespoons of the oil in a large skillet; fry the cakes until golden, about 5 minutes per side. Drain on paper towels; serve with sauce.

Nutrition information
Per serving: 354 calories, 19 g fat, 5 g saturated fat, 200 mg cholesterol, 27 g carbohydrates, 19 g protein, 578 mg sodium, 2 g fiber

Sauteed scallops with chermoula

Prep: 20 minutes   **Cook:** 5 minutes   **Makes:** 4 servings

This recipe is adapted from one served at T'afia restaurant in Houston and was included in a 2009 Dinner at Home column. The North African chermoula sauce also makes a fantastic dressing for romaine, chicken or shrimp salad.

Chermoula sauce:
4 cloves garlic
3/4 cup olive oil
1/2 cup each: parsley leaves, cilantro leaves
1/3 cup fresh lemon juice
1 teaspoon each: ground cumin, sweet or smoked paprika
3/4 teaspoon salt
1/4 teaspoon ground red pepper

Scallops:
1 ¼ pounds large sea scallops
1/4 teaspoon salt
Freshly ground pepper
2 tablespoons olive oil
Parsley sprigs

1 For chermoula sauce, process garlic, oil, parsley, cilantro, lemon juice, cumin, paprika, salt and ground red pepper in a blender until garlic and herbs are finely chopped. Taste; adjust seasonings. (Chermoula will keep up to 2 days covered in the refrigerator; use at room temperature.)

2 Pat scallops dry. Season with the salt and pepper to taste. Heat oil in large nonstick skillet over medium-high heat. Add the scallops in a single, uncrowded layer. Sear until golden, about 3 minutes. Turn; sear the other side, about 1 ½ minutes.

3 Transfer scallops and pan juices to 4 plates. Spoon about 2 tablespoons of the chermoula over and around each serving. Garnish with parsley sprigs.

Nutrition information
Per serving: 309 calories, 21 g fat, 3 g saturated fat, 47 mg cholesterol, 5 g carbohydrates, 24 g protein, 521 mg sodium, 0 g fiber

5
Pasta and Rice

Chicken penne with tomato-garlic cream sauce

Prep: 30 minutes   **Cooking:** 12 minutes   **Makes:** 6 servings

Former test kitchen chef Mark Graham created this simple yet elegant pasta for a 2003 story on planning a fall Italian dinner party. Use a rotisserie chicken, or roast your own.

1 pound penne pasta
2 tablespoons butter
1 onion, thinly sliced
1/2 teaspoon red pepper flakes
2 cloves garlic, minced
2 pounds plum tomatoes, seeded, chopped,
   or 1 can (28 ounces) diced tomatoes, drained
2 cups whipping cream or half-and-half
1 cup frozen peas
1/2 teaspoon salt
Freshly ground pepper
1 roasted chicken, about 2 pounds, skinned, meat
   shredded

1 Heat 4 quarts of salted water to a boil; add pasta. Return to a boil; cook until al dente, about 7 minutes. Drain, reserving 1/2 cup of the cooking liquid.

2 Meanwhile, melt butter in large skillet; stir in onion and red pepper flakes. Cook until softened, about 3 minutes. Stir in garlic; cook 1 minute. Stir in tomatoes, cream and reserved pasta cooking liquid. Increase heat to high; cook until slightly reduced, about 4 minutes. Stir in peas, salt, pepper to taste, cooked pasta and chicken; stir to coat evenly. Heat 4 minutes. Pour into large serving bowl.

Nutrition information
Per serving: 731 calories, 39 g fat, 22 g saturated fat, 168 mg cholesterol, 67 g carbohydrates, 29 g protein, 346 mg sodium, 6 g fiber

Macaroni and cheese with bacon and tomato

Prep: 25 minutes   **Cooking:** 1 hour   **Makes:** 8 servings

This recipe — developed in the test kitchen for a 2002 story about the upscale return of macaroni and cheese — adds color (from the tomatoes) and texture (from crisp bits of bacon) to the classic dish.

3/4 cup bread crumbs
1 package (1 pound) cavatappi or penne pasta
2 tablespoons unsalted butter
3 tablespoons flour
1/8 teaspoon nutmeg
1 quart milk
1/2 teaspoon each, or to taste: salt, freshly ground pepper
1/2 pound each, shredded: Gruyere cheese, processed cheese (such as Velveeta)
1 pound bacon, cooked, crumbled
3 ripe plum tomatoes, diced
3 tablespoons olive oil

1 Generously butter a 1 ½-quart baking dish. Add 1/4 cup of the bread crumbs; shake to coat dish evenly. Heat a large pot of salted water to a boil. Cook pasta until al dente, about 7 minutes. Drain. Place in large bowl.

2 Heat oven to 350 degrees. Melt butter in large saucepan over medium heat. Whisk in flour; cook, stirring, 2 minutes. Add nutmeg; cook 1 minute. Whisk in milk. Heat to a boil; reduce heat to simmer. Cook, stirring, 5 minutes. Season with salt and pepper. Remove from heat; stir in cheeses until melted.

3 Add sauce to pasta, mix well. Spoon 1/2 of the mixture into prepared baking dish. Add bacon and tomatoes in an even layer. Top with remaining macaroni mixture. Combine remaining 1/2 cup bread crumbs with olive oil in small bowl. Sprinkle over macaroni. Bake until golden and bubbly, 45 minutes.

Nutrition information
Per serving: 690 calories, 38 g fat, 18 g saturated fat, 90 mg cholesterol, 1,075 mg sodium, 56 g carbohydrate, 31 g protein, 2 g fiber

Goat cheese ravioli with sage and brown butter

Prep: 25 minutes   **Cooking:** 10 minutes   **Makes:** 3 servings

For a 2006 cover story on Illinois cheesemaker Leslie Cooperband and her farmstead dairy, former staff writer Robin Mather Jenkins developed this recipe to spotlight Cooperband's fresh goat cheese. She used Chinese won ton wrappers in place of pasta dough for the ravioli.

3 tablespoons butter
1/2 onion, minced
6 ounces fresh goat cheese
1 egg
1/2 teaspoon salt
Freshly ground pepper
30 won ton wrappers
13 to 15 fresh sage leaves plus 1/2 teaspoon
   minced sage
1 tablespoon vermouth or dry white wine

1 Heat the butter in a small skillet over medium heat. Add the onion; cook, stirring often, until translucent, about 2 minutes. Remove skillet from heat. Transfer 2 tablespoons of the onion from the skillet to a medium bowl. Add the goat cheese, egg, salt and pepper to taste to the bowl; mix well.

2 Wet one won ton wrapper with cold water with your fingers. Place 1 tablespoon of the cheese mixture on the center of the wrapper; place one sage leaf on top. Cover with another wet won ton wrapper; squeeze out as much air as possible. Press firmly to seal edges. If desired, use a biscuit cutter to cut into rounds. Repeat procedure until all the cheese mixture has been used, making 13 to 15 ravioli.

3 Heat a large pot of lightly salted water to a boil over high heat. Return the skillet with the remaining onions to the stove top over medium heat. Cook, stirring often, until onion and butter turn light brown, about 5 minutes. Remove skillet from heat; stir in vermouth and the minced sage.

4 Add 4 to 6 of the ravioli to the boiling water. Cook until they float to the surface, about 3-4 minutes. Remove ravioli from water; drain. Place in a shallow buttered dish. Repeat with remaining ravioli. Pour the browned butter and onions over the ravioli; serve hot.

Nutrition information
Per serving: 520 calories, 26 g fat, 16 g saturated fat, 134 mg cholesterol, 49 g carbohydrates, 21 g protein, 1,080 mg sodium, 2 g fiber

Smoky butternut and bacon risotto with ginger

Prep: 25 minutes   **Cooking:** 40 minutes   **Makes:** 6 servings

For faster preparation, substitute the peeled fresh squash found at some supermarkets and specialty markets. Shredded, cooked duck or chicken turns this hearty dish from a 2009 Dinner at Home column into company fare.

3 thick slices applewood smoked bacon, cut crosswise into matchstick-size strips

1 large sweet onion, diced

1/2 small butternut squash, peeled, halved, seeded, cut into 1/2-inch cubes

4 cloves garlic, finely chopped or crushed

1 teaspoon minced ginger root

5 cups chicken broth or stock

1/2 cup dry white wine or broth

1 teaspoon salt

1/2 teaspoon freshly ground pepper

2 cups arborio rice

2 cups shredded roasted duck or chicken, optional

1/2 cup finely grated aged cheese, such as manchego, smoked aged gouda, Parmesan

2 tablespoons chopped fresh chives or parsley or a combination

1 Place bacon in a Dutch oven; cook over medium-high heat until the fat is rendered and the strips are crisp, 7 minutes. Remove the bacon with a slotted spoon to drain on paper towels. Add the onion and squash to the bacon fat; cook, stirring often, until tender, 8 minutes. Stir in the garlic and ginger; cook 1 minute.

2 Meanwhile, heat the broth, wine, salt and pepper in a saucepan to a simmer. Stir rice into squash mixture; cook, stirring, over medium heat to coat the grains of rice with the fat, 1 minute. Stir in 2 cups of the broth mixture; cook over medium-high heat until the broth comes to a simmer. Reduce heat to keep the broth at a gentle simmer. Cook, stirring often, until most of the liquid has been absorbed, about 8 minutes. Add another 1/2 cup of the broth. Simmer gently, stirring until it is absorbed, 5 minutes. Continue simmering and adding broth, 1/2 cup at a time, until the rice is just tender but not hard in the interior, 12-15 minutes.

3 Stir in the shredded duck or chicken, cheese and chives. Serve in wide bowls; sprinkle each serving with the bacon and more cheese, if desired.

Nutrition information
Per serving: 387 calories, 10 g fat, 3 g saturated fat, 9 mg cholesterol, 62 g carbohydrates, 14 g protein, 1,213 mg sodium, 4 g fiber

Fennel risotto cakes

Prep: 1 hour **Cooking:** 2 hours **Cool:** 30 minutes **Makes:** 8 servings

This recipe for risotto cakes appeared with a 2004 story about the small plates trend in Chicago restaurants. It's from chef/co-owner Shawn McClain, of the vegetarian restaurant Green Zebra.

1 large fennel bulb, 3⁄4 of bulb minced, 1⁄4 thinly sliced
2 cups red wine
1/2 cup port
2 tablespoons sugar
3 tablespoons extra-virgin olive oil
1 onion, minced
3 cloves garlic, minced
1 ½ cups arborio rice
1/2 cup licorice-flavored liqueur such as anisette, ouzo or sambuca
2 cans (14 ½ ounces each) vegetable broth
1/2 cup finely grated Parmesan cheese
2 tablespoons mascarpone cheese
1 tablespoon fennel pollen, optional, see note
3 cups bread crumbs
1/2 teaspoon salt
Freshly ground pepper
1 tablespoon butter

1 Heat oven to 250 degrees. Roast the fennel slices until golden brown, about 30 minutes. Meanwhile, heat red wine, port and sugar in a non-reactive saucepan over medium heat until it becomes syrupy, about 45 minutes. Remove from heat.

2 Heat 2 tablespoons of the oil in a medium skillet over medium heat. Add minced fennel, onion and garlic; cook until onion is translucent, about 5 minutes. Add rice; reduce heat to medium-low. Cook, stirring, 1 minute. Add liqueur; cook until liquid evaporates, about 5 minutes.

3 Meanwhile, heat vegetable broth in a medium saucepan over medium-high heat just to a simmer; remove from heat. Add one-third of the warm vegetable stock to the rice. Cook, stirring, until liquid is absorbed into the rice, about 10 minutes. Repeat two more times until rice feels soft but not mushy, about 30 minutes total cooking time. (You may need a little more vegetable stock if the rice is still firm.) Remove rice from heat; fold in Parmesan, mascarpone and fennel pollen. Spread rice in one layer on a baking sheet; cool, about 30 minutes.

4 Heat oven to 350 degrees. Place bread crumbs in a large pan or plate. Form cooled rice into 8 small balls with your hands. Flatten balls; coat on all sides with bread crumbs. Heat remaining 1 tablespoon of the olive oil in large skillet; cook cakes until golden, in batches if necessary, turning once, about 3 minutes each side. Return cooked cakes to baking sheet. Season with salt and pepper. Bake until crisp and deep golden, about 4 minutes.

5 Meanwhile, heat wine sauce over medium heat in saucepan until heated through, about 2 minutes. Whisk in butter. Serve with cakes.

Note
Fennel pollen, harvested from fennel flowers, has an intense sweetness. It is sold in spice stores or online.

Nutrition information
Per serving: 440 calories, 12 g fat, 4 g saturated fat, 13 mg cholesterol, 69 g carbohydrates, 12 g protein, 972 mg sodium, 4 g fiber

6
Salads and Sides

Napa slaw with charred salmon

Prep: 1 hour   **Cooking:** 10 minutes   **Makes:** 4 servings

This recipe, perfect for a lunch or light dinner, appeared in a summer 2002 story about the many guises of coleslaw. It is from chef Michael Altenberg, of Bistro Campagne.

3 shallots, coarsely chopped
3 tablespoons Champagne vinegar
  or white wine vinegar
2 tablespoons dark brown or turbinado sugar
1/2 teaspoon sea salt
Cracked pepper, three-color peppercorns preferred
1 head napa cabbage, thinly sliced
1 bulb onion or 4 green onions (white only),
  chopped
1 each, cut into matchsticks: red and yellow
  bell pepper
1 carrot, peeled, cut into matchsticks
1 fillet (8 ounces) salmon
Salt and pepper to taste
1 to 2 tablespoons Dijon mustard
2 tablespoons olive oil

1 Combine shallots, vinegar and sugar in a blender; puree until smooth. Add salt and pepper to taste. Combine with cabbage, onion, bell peppers and carrot in a large bowl; toss. Taste for seasoning. Set aside.

2 Prepare a grill or heat a grill pan or broiler. Season salmon with salt and pepper. Grill 4 minutes; turn. Grill 3 minutes; brush salmon with a thin film of mustard with a pastry brush. Turn; cook about 45 seconds. Brush with mustard; turn. Cook until medium-rare and lightly charred, about 1 minute. Spread slaw on a serving platter. Flake salmon; scatter over the slaw. Drizzle olive oil over salad.

Nutrition information
Per serving: 255 calories, 12 g fat, 2 g saturated fat, 35 mg cholesterol, 450 mg sodium, 23 g carbohydrate, 17 g protein, 2 g fiber

Editor's Tip: Napa cabbage also is called Chinese cabbage. It has a mild flavor and an elongated, pale green head. Be sure to cut off the base and wash the leaves thoroughly. For this recipe, you also can use red or green cabbage.

Shrimp salad with creamy pepper-citrus dressing

Prep: 15 minutes   **Makes:** 4 main-dish servings

This main dish salad, featured in a 2003 summer Dinner Tonight column, is easy to assemble, and the major preparation time is devoted to the salad dressing.

1/2 cup low-fat or regular mayonnaise
3 tablespoons orange juice
Juice of 1 lime
1 tablespoon honey
2 teaspoons white wine vinegar
2 teaspoons minced fresh tarragon
   or 1 teaspoon dried
1/2 teaspoon salt
1/4 teaspoon ground red pepper
Freshly ground black pepper
1 bag (9 ounces) pre-cut mixed salad greens
16 cherry or grape tomatoes, halved
 1 green bell pepper, sliced
3 green onions, chopped
20 large shrimp, shelled, cooked

1 Whisk together mayonnaise, orange and lime juices, honey and vinegar in small bowl until well blended. Add tarragon, salt and peppers to taste.

2 Combine lettuce, tomatoes, bell pepper and green onions in large salad bowl. Top with shrimp. Toss with the dressing.

Nutrition information
Per serving: 181 calories, 7 g fat, 1 g saturated fat, 0 mg cholesterol, 23 g carbohydrates, 14 g protein, 1,218 mg sodium, 10 g fiber

Warm salad of beef with avocado-mango salsa

Prep: 25 minutes   **Cooking:** 7 minutes   **Makes:** 2 main-course servings

With his 2006 Prep School column about making emulsions, freelance writer James P. DeWan offered this recipe for readers to apply the newly learned technique of making vinaigrette. The "warm salad" name comes from the Australian term for dishes featuring hot meat on top of greens.

1 rib-eye, New York strip or sirloin steak,
  about 8 ounces
1/8 teaspoon coarse salt
Freshly ground pepper

Vinaigrette and greens:
1 tablespoon sherry vinegar or other vinegar
1 teaspoon Dijon mustard
1/4 teaspoon coarse salt
3 tablespoons extra-virgin olive oil
1 teaspoon honey
8 ounces mesclun mix or other fresh salad greens

Avocado-mango salsa:
2 cloves garlic, minced
1 each, peeled, cut into medium dice: avocado, mango
1/4 red onion, cut into small dice
2 tablespoons extra-virgin olive oil
1 tablespoon minced cilantro
1/2 teaspoon each: coarse salt, ground cumin
1/4 teaspoon each: freshly ground pepper, dried
  oregano
Juice of 1 lime, hot red pepper sauce

1 Season steak with salt and pepper to taste. Grill, saute or broil to medium-rare, about 3 ½ minutes per side. Remove from heat; let rest 10 minutes.

2 Meanwhile, for the vinaigrette, whisk the vinegar, mustard and salt in a small bowl; whisk in a few drops of oil to form an emulsion. Continue whisking while adding remaining oil in a slow, steady stream; whisk in honey. Toss greens with vinaigrette.

3 Combine salsa ingredients in a medium bowl; set aside. Divide dressed greens between plates; mound salsa in center. Slice steak on the diagonal into thin strips; fan out across top of salsa.

Nutrition information
Per serving: 714 calories, 55 g fat, 9 g saturated fat, 60 mg cholesterol, 39 g carbohydrates, 24 g protein, 953 mg sodium, 12 g fiber

Bitter greens with bacon, pecans and warm balsamic dressing

Prep: 30 minutes   **Cooking:** 10 minutes   **Makes:** 4 servings

This salad was developed by former staff writer Emily Nunn for our "Columbian Exchange" special section, celebrating Columbus Day. The recipe was inspired by one in Lynn Rosetto Kasper's "The Splendid Table," plus the memory of a recipe in an old issue of Metropolitan Home magazine.

4 to 5 slices bacon, cut crosswise
   into 1/2-inch pieces
1 cup pecan halves
1/4 cup extra-virgin olive oil
2 large cloves garlic, chopped
2 shallots, halved lengthwise, sliced
   into 1/4-inch slices
1/2 teaspoon salt
1/8 teaspoon freshly ground pepper
1/4 cup balsamic vinegar
3 tablespoons red wine vinegar
1 to 2 tablespoons brown sugar
8 cups mixed bitter greens (arugula, radicchio, endive)

1 Cook bacon in a medium skillet over medium-high heat until crisp; remove to a paper towel-lined plate. Cool; crumble. Remove all but 1/4 cup of the bacon grease in the skillet; add pecans. Cook, stirring, until fragrant, being careful not to burn, about 1 minute. Remove with slotted spoon to paper towel.

2 Add olive oil to skillet; heat over medium heat. Add garlic, shallots, salt and pepper; cook until garlic and shallots are softened, 1-2 minutes. Add the vinegars and brown sugar; cook until dressing comes to a boil, about 2 minutes. Adjust seasonings. Place greens, pecans and bacon in a salad bowl; drizzle with dressing to taste.

Nutrition information
Per serving: 389 calories, 36 g fat, 4 g saturated fat, 7 mg cholesterol, 14 g carbohydrates, 6 g protein, 455 mg sodium, 3 g fiber

Favorite things summer salad

Prep: 15 minutes **Cooking:** 12 minutes **Makes:** 4 servings

"Consider this a warning before adding this main-course salad to your repertoire," wrote former test kitchen director Donna Pierce in a summer 2004 Dinner Tonight column. "The lightly fried, flat nuts from Spain known as marcona almonds are completely addictive — and one of the delicious reasons this salad has become a weekly routine at my house." Look for marcona nuts at specialty markets, or substitute regular roasted almonds.

Vinaigrette:
1 tablespoon sherry wine vinegar
1 shallot, chopped
1 teaspoon Dijon mustard
3 tablespoons olive oil

Salad:
2 boneless chicken breast halves
1/4 teaspoon salt
Freshly ground pepper
6 cups mixed baby greens
1 ½ ounces Manchego cheese, very thinly sliced
12 pitted black olives, halved
4 anchovy fillets, chopped
1 avocado, halved, pitted
4 eggs, hard-cooked, peeled, quartered
12 cherry tomatoes, halved
1/4 cup Marcona or roasted almonds, coarsely chopped

1 Heat a grill or grill pan to high. For vinaigrette, whisk together vinegar, shallot and mustard in a medium bowl; whisk in oil. Set aside.

2 Season chicken breast with salt and pepper. Grill, turning once, until golden and cooked through, about 18 minutes. Remove from grill; cool. Slice.

3 Meanwhile, toss together lettuce, cheese, olives and anchovies in a large bowl. Divide lettuce mixture among plates. Remove avocado flesh from shell by sliding a spoon around shell; slice thinly.

4 Garnish salads evenly with avocado, eggs, tomatoes and almonds; top with chicken slices. Whisk dressing to blend; drizzle dressing evenly over salads.

Nutrition information
Per serving: 459 calories, 34 g fat, 7 g saturated fat, 262 mg cholesterol, 13 g carbohydrates, 28 g protein, 590 mg sodium, 6 g fiber

Spinach and fingerling potato salad with warm bacon dressing

Prep: 20 minutes   **Cooking:** 25 minutes   **Makes:** 6 servings

In a 2002 story "Back to bacon," we described how the breakfast staple had renewed its image with new artisan brands. Accompanying the story was this appealing salad with a warm vinaigrette dressing, developed in the test kitchen.

1/2 pound each: fingerling potatoes, thick-cut bacon
2 large shallots, minced
1/2 cup olive oil
1/4 cup red wine vinegar
2 tablespoons maple syrup
2 teaspoons minced orange zest
1/2 teaspoon each: salt, freshly ground pepper
1/2 pound baby spinach
1/2 cup pine nuts, toasted, see note

1 Heat a large pot of salted water to a boil; add pota-toes. Cook until potatoes are tender, 10-15 minutes. Drain; let cool until just warm. Cut into 1/4-inch slices; set aside.

2 Cook bacon in a skillet over medium-low heat until just crisp, 8 minutes. Drain bacon on paper towels. Let cool. Chop or crumble into bits; set aside. Pour off all but 1 tablespoon of the fat from the skillet. Place over medium-high heat; add shallots. Cook until golden, 1 minute.

3 Mix bacon, shallots, olive oil, vinegar, maple syrup and orange zest in a small microwave-safe bowl. Season with salt and pepper. Heat in microwave until warm, about 30 seconds. Toss potatoes and spinach in large bowl with dressing. Garnish with pine nuts.

Note
To toast pine nuts, place in a dry skillet over medium-low heat. Cook, stirring occasionally, until golden brown, 1-2 minutes. Watch carefully to avoid burning.

Nutrition information
Per serving: 350 calories, 30 g fat, 6 g saturated fat, 11 mg cholesterol, 8 g protein, 13 g carbohydrate, 420 mg sodium, 2 g fiber

Tarragon egg salad

Prep: 10 minutes **Makes:** about 2 cups

We saluted that classic all-American condiment, mayonnaise, in a July 2008 story and included this egg salad recipe. Use it to make sandwiches or serve it on a bed of lettuce garnished with shrimp or lobster.

    2 tablespoons each: mayonnaise, sour cream
    1 tablespoon each, freshly minced: tarragon leaves,
      flat-leaf parsley
    2 teaspoons each: Dijon-style mustard, fresh lemon juice
    1 ½ teaspoons each: celery seed, salt
    Freshly ground pepper
    6 hard-cooked eggs, peeled, mashed or chopped

Mix together the mayonnaise, sour cream, tarragon, parsley, mustard, lemon juice, celery seed, salt and pepper to taste in a medium bowl. Stir in the eggs.

Nutrition information
Per 1/2 cup serving: 187 calories, 15 g fat, 4 g saturated fat, 324 mg cholesterol, 2 g carbohydrates, 10 g protein, 1,028 mg sodium, 0 g fiber

Editor's Tip: Here's a sure-fire way to cook eggs for egg salad: Gently place raw eggs into softly boiling water (over medium heat) with a large spoon; cook 12 minutes. Cool under running water about 2 minutes. Peel.

French bean salad with hazelnuts, tomato and honey-crème fraiche dressing

Prep: 20 minutes   **Cooking:** 5 minutes   **Makes:** 4 servings

A 2003 story about artisanal honeys included this recipe, adapted from one by chef Martial Noguier, then executive chef of one sixtyblue restaurant. Look for the honeys in specialty food shops or natural food stores.

1 pound French or other green beans, trimmed
1/4 cup creme fraiche
1 tablespoon tomato juice
2 teaspoons red wine vinegar
1 teaspoon tupelo or linden honey
1/4 teaspoon each: salt, ground red pepper
1/2 cup roasted hazelnuts, see note
2 plum tomatoes, seeded, diced
1/4 cup finely chopped chives
4 basil leaves

1 Fill large saucepan with salted water; heat over high heat to a boil. Stir in beans; cook until tender, about 5 minutes. Drain; plunge into ice water to stop cooking. Drain; set aside

2 Whisk together creme fraiche, tomato juice, red wine vinegar, honey, salt and red pepper in a small bowl; set aside.

3 Toss together beans, hazelnuts, diced tomatoes and chopped chives in a large bowl; add the dressing to the vegetables. Toss; divide into four salad bowls. Garnish with basil leaves.

Note
Toast hazelnuts over low heat in a small, dry skillet, stirring constantly, until fragrant, about 5 minutes. Rub between towels to remove skins.

Nutrition information
Per serving: 168 calories, 12 g fat, 3 g saturated fat, 6 mg cholesterol, 12 g carbohydrates, 4 g protein, 575 mg sodium, 5 g fiber

Spinach and chanterelles in nutmeg sauce

Prep: 10 minutes   Cooking: 20 minutes   Makes: 4 servings

A sprinkling of nutmeg is what gives creamed spinach its distinctive taste. This version was developed in our test kitchen for a story on nutmeg in our 2001 "On the Spice Trail" series. For a lighter version, use only about half of the cream.

1/2 stick (4 tablespoons) unsalted butter
1 onion, chopped
1 clove garlic, minced
1 tablespoon flour
3/4 cup each: chicken broth, whipping cream
2 tablespoons grated Parmesan cheese
1/2 teaspoon each: ground nutmeg,
    pepper
Salt to taste
1/2 pound fresh chanterelle or other mushrooms,
    sliced
1 ½ pounds baby spinach

1 Melt 2 tablespoons of the butter in saucepan over medium-high heat. Cook onion and garlic, stirring, until soft and golden, 3 minutes. Sprinkle flour over; cook, stirring, until thickened, 1 minute.

2 Turn heat to high; whisk in chicken broth until smooth. Cook until reduced by half, 5 minutes. Reduce heat to medium; stir in cream, cheese, nutmeg, pepper and salt to taste. Set aside.

3 Melt remaining 2 tablespoons of the butter in large skillet over medium-high heat. Cook mushrooms until soft, about 1 minute. Add spinach; cook, stirring, until spinach is soft and liquid from vegetables has evaporated, 6 minutes. Stir cream sauce into vegetables; heat to a simmer. Cook 3 minutes. Adjust seasonings.

Nutrition information
Per serving: 340 calories, 30 g fat, 18 g saturated fat, 95 mg cholesterol, 320 mg sodium, 13 g carbohydrate, 9 g protein, 5 g fiber

Sesame bok choy, yellow peppers and onions

Prep: 15 minutes **Cooking:** 6 minutes **Makes:** 6 servings

A July 2006 story about cooking in a wok proclaimed it the original non-stick pan: versatile, durable and fun to use. It's the only pan you really need, declared Food Editor Carol Mighton Haddix, who developed this dish to showcase the wok's many attributes.

2 tablespoons peanut oil
6 heads baby bok choy, each cut in 2-inch pieces
2 yellow bell peppers, halved, seeded, cut in strips
1 red onion, sliced
1/4 cup soy sauce or tamari
1 teaspoon toasted sesame oil
Freshly ground pepper
1/4 cup chopped cilantro

Heat oil in a wok over high heat. Add bok choy; stir-fry 2 minutes. Add the bell peppers and onion; stir-fry 2 more minutes. Add soy sauce, sesame oil and pepper to taste; cook, tossing to coat vegetables, 2 minutes. Transfer to a platter; garnish with cilantro.

Nutrition information
Per serving: 190 calories, 5 g fat, 0 g saturated fat, 55 mg cholesterol, 31 g carbohydrates, 8 g protein, 945 mg sodium, 4 g fiber

Editor's Tip: This is a versatile recipe. Almost any type of vegetable lends itself to stir-frying. Try this same method with broccoli or cauliflower florets, green onions and hot chilies, if you like them. Or mix diagonally cut zucchini and carrots with sliced shallots.

Giardiniera

Prep: 1 hour **Cooking:** 2 1/2 days **Makes:** 3 cups

We included this recipe for giardiniera, a spicy Italian relish, in a 2007 "What's Your Dish?" column after a reader wrote to request one. The giardiniera will keep in the refrigerator for several weeks. Use it to top sandwiches or burgers or as a topping for salads or roast meats.

6 jalapeno chilies, thinly sliced
2 each, diced: green and red bell peppers
1 each, diced: celery rib, carrot, yellow onion
1/2 head cauliflower, cut into florets
1/2 cup salt
3 cloves garlic, minced
1/2 cup chopped stuffed green olives
2 ½ teaspoons dried oregano
1/2 to 1 teaspoon red pepper flakes
1/2 teaspoon celery seeds
Freshly ground black pepper
1 cup each: apple cider vinegar, extra-virgin olive oil

1 Combine the jalapenos, bell peppers, celery, carrot, onion and cauliflower florets in a large bowl; stir in the salt. Add cold water to cover vegetables; cover bowl. Refrigerate 12 hours. Drain salt water; rinse vegetables. Set aside in the bowl.

2 Combine the garlic, olives, oregano, red pepper flakes, celery seeds and black pepper to taste in a small bowl; set aside.

3 Pour the vinegar into a medium bowl; whisk in the seasonings. Whisk in the olive oil. Pour over the vegetable mixture; toss lightly. Cover; refrigerate at least 48 hours before using.

Nutrition information
Per tablespoon: 49 calories, 5 g fat, 1 g saturated fat, 0 mg cholesterol, 2 g carbohydrates, 0 g protein, 300 mg sodium, 1 g fiber

7
Desserts

Corner Bakery French toast

Prep: 15 minutes   **Cook:** 50 minutes   **Makes:** 6 servings

A reader requested a recipe for this restaurant chain's "French toast," which is really a wonderfully rich, soft and moist bread pudding that's sturdy enough to slice into squares for dessert. For a crunch, sprinkle chopped pecans or walnuts over the bottom layer of bread. Use whole milk in place of the whipping cream for a lighter version.

14 thick slices day-old bakery cinnamon-raisin bread
3 eggs
1 ½ cups half-and-half
1 cup whipping cream
1/2 cup sugar
1/2 teaspoon each: vanilla, ground cinnamon
Maple syrup, warmed, optional

1 Heat oven to 375 degrees. Line bottom of greased 8-inch square baking pan with 3 slices of bread, cutting to fit; top with 3 more slices, cutting to fit. Place 8 slices across top in 2 rows, shingle-fashion. Press down firmly.

2 Whisk eggs in medium bowl; whisk in half-and-half, cream, sugar, vanilla and cinnamon. Pour egg mixture evenly over bread. Cover tightly with foil. Bake 40 minutes. Remove foil; bake 10 minutes. Let stand 10 minutes before serving. Serve with maple syrup if you like.

Nutrition information
Per serving: 535 calories, 27g fat, 14 g saturated fat, 180 mg cholesterol, 59 g carbohydrates, 14 g protein, 355 mg sodium, 2.8 g fiber

Strawberry shortcake muffins

Prep: 20 minutes   **Cook:** 15 minutes   **Makes:** 12 muffins

For a 2003 story on kitchen chemistry, we developed this delicious strawberry muffin recipe. Any type of berries may be used.

2 cups flour
1/2 cup sugar
2 teaspoons baking powder
1/2 teaspoon salt
1 cup milk
1 egg, slightly beaten
1/2 cup melted butter
12 strawberries, sliced

1 Heat oven to 425 degrees. Combine the flour, 1/4 cup of the sugar, baking powder and salt in a large bowl. Stir in milk, egg and butter, stirring only enough to dampen all the flour; the batter should not be smooth.

2 Spoon into buttered muffin cups, filling each about 2/3 full. Press 3-4 strawberry slices into batter in each cup, pointed side up. Sprinkle each muffin with 1 teaspoon of the remaining sugar. Bake until golden, 15-18 minutes

Nutrition information
Per muffin: 160 calories, 5 g fat, 3 g saturated fat, 30 mg cholesterol, 230 mg sodium, 26 g carbohydrate, 4 g protein, 1 g fiber

Editor's Tip: The key to making light muffins is not beating the batter. Simply stir the ingredients together lightly, just to moisten the flour. Lumps are perfectly OK and will disappear during baking.

Babka

Prep: 35 minutes   **Stand:** 3 hours, 20 minutes   **Cook:** 50 minutes   **Makes:** 12 servings

Dobra Bielinski of Delightful Pastries bakery in Chicago shared this recipe with Good Eating for a 2007 Easter story on the traditional Polish yeast cake.

Dough:
1/4 cup very warm water (105-115 degrees)
1 package (1/4 ounce) active dry yeast
   or 1 piece (1/2 ounce) fresh yeast
1/2 cup plus 1 teaspoon sugar
3 ½ cups flour
6 egg yolks
1 ½ sticks (3/4 cup) unsalted butter,
   melted, cooled
1/4 cup milk
1/2 teaspoon salt
Finely grated zest of 2 lemons
1 cup raisins
1/2 cup candied orange peel, see note

Soaking syrup:
1 cup water
1/2 cup each: sugar, rum
1 teaspoon vanilla

Glaze:
1 cup confectioners' sugar, sifted
1 to 3 tablespoons water
Raisins, candied orange peel,
   optional

1 For the dough, mix the water, yeast, 1 teaspoon of the sugar and 1/4 cup of the flour in a bowl with electric mixer (fitted with a paddle, if you have one). Sprinkle another 1/4 cup of the flour on top of the mixture. Let mixture stand until it rises and cracks on the sides, about 45 minutes.

2 Change the mixer paddle to a dough hook; add the egg yolks, butter, remaining 1/2 cup of the sugar, milk and salt. Mix until blended together. Add 1/4 cup of the flour, mixing to a smooth consistency. Set aside 1/2 cup of the flour. Add remaining flour slowly, mixing until dough is silky and smooth, about 2 minutes. If the dough is smooth and comes away from the sides of the bowl, do not add more flour. If dough is wet, add the reserved flour. Stir in the lemon zest, raisins and orange peel. Transfer dough to a floured surface; knead into a round ball. Allow to rest 10 minutes.

3 Shape the dough into a tire shape in a well-greased kugelhopf pan or tube pan. Cover with a kitchen towel; let rest in a warm, draft-free place until dough rises to 1/4 inch below the top of the pan, about 2 hours.

4 Heat oven to 325 degrees. Bake the cake until an inserted tester tests clean, 45-60 minutes. (Cover with foil if it browns too quickly.) Remove the cake from the mold; transfer to a baking sheet. Return to the oven until cake browns completely on all sides, about 5-10 minutes. Let cool on a wire rack 15 minutes.

5 Meanwhile, for the soaking syrup, heat the water and sugar to a boil in a medium saucepan over medium-high heat. Cook until sugar dissolves, about 1 minute; remove from heat. Add rum and vanilla; pour into a bowl big enough to hold the cake. Place the cake in the bowl with the syrup. Carefully rotate the cake to coat all sides with syrup; remove to the baking sheet. Let stand 10 minutes before glazing, allowing the rum syrup to slowly penetrate.

6 For the glaze, whisk the confectioners' sugar with water to desired consistency. Drizzle the glaze over the top of the cake; sprinkle with raisins and candied orange peel. Slice with a serrated knife.

Note
Candied orange peel is available in the baking section of some specialty markets.

Nutrition information
Per serving: 438 calories, 14 g fat, 8 g saturated fat, 133 mg cholesterol, 74 g carbohydrates, 6 g protein, 118 mg sodium, 2 g fiber

Pumpkin flan with gingersnap crust

Prep: 20 minutes   **Cook:** 1 hour, 25 minutes   **Chill:** 8 hours   **Makes:** 8 servings

A 2006 Thanksgiving story took on a Latin theme, featuring bold and spicy flavors. This dessert from chef Douglas Rodriguez, of the former DeLaCosta restaurant, drew raves from tasters. "The pumpkin flan tastes like pumpkin pie, Latino style," he said. He uses fresh pumpkin, but 15 ounces of canned pureed pumpkin can be substituted.

1/2 small pumpkin, about 8 ounces, peeled, seeded, cut into 2-inch chunks
1 can (14 ounces) condensed milk
1 can (12 ounces) evaporated milk
8 eggs
1 cup plus 3 tablespoons sugar
1 box (16 ounces) gingersnap cookies
1 stick (1/2 cup) butter, melted

1 Cover pumpkin with water in a medium saucepan; heat to a simmer over high heat. Cook until fork-tender, about 15 minutes; drain. Transfer pumpkin to a food processor; add condensed and evaporated milks, eggs and 3 tablespoons of the sugar. Puree until smooth; set aside.

2 Heat remaining 1 cup of the sugar in a saucepan over medium heat; cook, stirring, until it becomes a light amber color, about 20 minutes. Pour the caramel into a 9-by-5-inch loaf pan. Pour in the puree.

3 Heat the oven to 350 degrees. Place the loaf pan in a deep baking dish partially filled with water. Bake until the flan is set, about 50 minutes. Remove the custard from the oven; cool completely on a wire rack.

4 Combine the cookies and melted butter in a food processor; pulse until well blended. Pack the mixture onto the cooled flan; refrigerate at least 8 hours. Run a small knife along edges of the mold to loosen; invert onto a serving platter.

Nutrition information
Per serving: 730 calories, 27 g fat, 13 g saturated fat, 262 mg cholesterol, 107 g carbohydrates, 17 g protein, 633 mg sodium, 1 g fiber

Editor's Tip: Try this recipe with other squash, such as butternut or Hubbard, or with sweet potatoes. For a more traditional pumpkin pie flavor, add pinches of ground cinnamon, ginger, nutmeg and cloves to the flan mixture. Another variation? Chocolate wafer cookies instead of gingersnaps for the crust.

Chocolate peanut butter pots de crème

Prep: 45 minutes   **Cook:** 40 minutes   **Chill:** 2 hours   **Makes:** 6 servings

When food editor Carol Mighton Haddix saw this recipe from chef Randal Jacobs, of Elate restaurant in Chicago, she just had to use it in 2010's Halloween section. Chef Jacobs serves the custard in oversize coffee cups, but you also can use ramekins.

1 ½ cups whipping cream
1/2 cup milk
1 ½ tablespoons sugar
5 egg yolks, beaten
5 ounces milk chocolate
2 cups chopped chocolate peanut butter cups, such as Reese's
1 vanilla bean
1/2 teaspoon sea salt, about
4 mint leaves, torn into pieces

1 Heat oven to 350 degrees. Combine 1 ¼ cups of the cream, the milk and 1 tablespoon of the sugar in a small saucepan; heat almost to a boil. In a bowl, whisk a little of the hot mixture into the egg yolks just to warm them; whisk the egg-yolk mixture back into the remaining milk-cream mixture. Add milk chocolate; let melt, about 1 minute. Whisk to incorporate.

2 Put mixture through a fine-mesh strainer; divide among six ramekins. Top with 1 ½ cups of the chopped peanut butter cups. Place ramekins in a large baking pan. Fill the pan with hot water to the same height as the mixture in the ramekins. Cover with foil; bake until set, about 35 minutes. Remove ramekins from the pan; top with remaining 1/2 cup of the peanut butter cups; let cool. Refrigerate 2 hours.

3 Beat remaining 1/4 cup of the cream and 1/2 tablespoon of the sugar in a bowl until stiff peaks form. Slice vanilla bean lengthwise; scrape out the pulp. Mix with sea salt. Place a dollop of whipped cream on each pot de creme; garnish with vanilla salt and mint leaves.

Nutrition information
Per serving: 629 calories, 47 g fat, 24 g saturated fat, 262 mg cholesterol, 46 g carbohydrates, 11 g protein, 1,862 mg sodium, 2 g fiber

Lemon meringue tart

Prep: 40 minutes   **Chill:** 5 hours or overnight   **Cook:** 30 minutes   **Makes:** 8 servings

Freelance writer Matt McMillen took up the case for lemon cream in a 2002 article. "Making lemon cream is for pastry-phobes and -philes alike. There are few recipes as simple and as fail-safe and as sublime," he wrote.

Tart dough:
1 stick (1/2 cup) butter, softened
1/4 cup sugar
1 egg yolk
1/2 teaspoon vanilla
1 cup plus 2 tablespoons flour
1/8 teaspoon salt

Lemon cream:
1 cup sugar
Zest of 4 lemons, finely chopped
4 eggs, lightly beaten
3/4 cup fresh lemon juice
2 ½ sticks (1 ¼ cups) butter,
    softened, cut into small pieces

Meringue:
3 large egg whites
3/4 cup sugar
1/4 teaspoon cream of tartar

1 For dough, beat butter with sugar in bowl of electric mixer until fluffy. Mix in egg yolk and vanilla. Slowly mix in flour and salt just to combine. Remove dough to floured surface; knead dough by hand briefly until flour and butter are fully combined. Wrap tightly with plastic wrap. Chill dough at least 1 hour. (The dough can be frozen up to a month. Let thaw in refrigerator overnight before using.)

2 Heat oven to 350 degrees. Roll out the dough 1/8-inch thick on a lightly floured surface; place in 10-inch tart pan. Trim any overhanging edges. Place in the freezer at least 15 minutes. Prick the surface with a fork; line with greased aluminum foil. Fill the shell with weights or dried beans. Bake 5 minutes. Remove the weights and foil; return to the oven. Bake until a light golden brown, 7 minutes. Let cool.

3 For lemon cream, place the sugar and zest in a double boiler set over simmering water; stir to mix. Heat until aromatic, about 2 minutes. Add eggs and lemon juice. Heat, stirring constantly, until temperature reaches 175 degrees and mixture is thick, about 10 minutes. Remove from heat; let cool, stirring occasionally, to 140 degrees, about 10 minutes. Transfer mixture to container of a blender or food processor. Turn on the blender; add the butter a couple of pieces at a time. Blend 3-5 minutes to fully emulsify. (Use at once or store in the refrigerator for up to 4 days or in the freezer for one month.) Refrigerate in bowl 4 hours or overnight.

4 For meringue, combine egg whites, sugar and cream of tartar in a stainless-steel bowl of electric mixer; place over a pan of simmering water. Do not let the water touch the bottom of the pan. Whisk the eggs constantly until sugar melts completely and whites are frothy and hot to the touch, about 3 minutes. Remove from the heat; whip on high speed until the whites are glossy and hold stiff peaks. Reduce speed to medium; whip until the egg whites have cooled to room temperature, about 5 minutes.

5 Heat broiler. Fill the cooked tart shell with lemon cream; smooth the surface. Spread meringue over the surface in a thick, even layer, making sure that the meringue covers all of the lemon cream and attaches to the crust to form a seal. Make a pattern of peaks and swirls with the back of a spoon. Place under the broiler until meringue is lightly browned, about 2 minutes.

Nutrition information

Per serving: 670 calories, 44 g fat, 26 g saturated fat, 240 mg cholesterol, 65 g carbohydrates, 7 g protein, 500 mg sodium, 1 g fiber

Butterscotch praline ice cream sundae

Prep: 15 minutes   **Cook:** 12 minutes   **Yield:** 6 sundaes

Vanilla ice cream is, for many of us, "a lifelong obsession, a romance that never gets stale," we wrote in a July 2002 article. Included was this deliciously decadent recipe from Heather Terhune, then executive chef at Atwood Cafe in Chicago.

Butterscotch sauce:

1 stick (1/2 cup) unsalted butter
1 ¼ cups packed brown sugar
3/4 cup each: light corn syrup, whipping cream
2 teaspoons vanilla
1 ¼ teaspoons salt

Candied pecans:

12 ounces whole pecans
4 tablespoons each: granulated sugar, melted butter
1 teaspoon salt

Ice cream:

1 quart premium vanilla ice cream
Whipped cream, optional

1 Heat oven to 350 degrees. For sauce, put butter, brown sugar, corn syrup, cream, vanilla and salt into a heavy saucepan over medium-high heat. Cook, whisking constantly, until it boils. Boil, uncovered, 2 minutes. Cool to room temperature, whisking occasionally so butter does not separate. (Sauce may be made ahead and refrigerated for up to 1 week.)

2 For pecans, put nuts, granulated sugar, butter and salt into a stainless-steel bowl; toss until thoroughly coated. Place on cookie sheet; bake until golden brown, about 10 minutes. Do not overbake. Cool.

3 Scoop ice cream into 6 bowls. Top with about 1/3 cup of the butterscotch sauce, a few candied pecans and whipped cream.

Nutrition information

Per serving: 1,200 calories, 85 g fat, 31 g saturated fat, 140 mg cholesterol, 1,100 mg sodium, 114 g carbohydrate, 9 g protein, 5 g fiber

Lychee Champagne granita

Prep: 10 minutes   **Freeze:** Overnight   **Yield:** 4 servings

For a 2009 story about Chinese New Year, chef Ming Tsai shared this granita using lychee fruit and Champagne (you can use any sparkling wine). Look for the fresh, sweet lychees in Chinese markets, or use the canned versions available in most supermarkets. For a different flavor, try canned apricots in place of the lychees.

1 can (15 ounces) lychees, 3/4 cup syrup reserved
1 tablespoon lemon juice
1 ½ cups sparkling wine, plus more for serving
4 whole fresh or canned lychees, optional

1 Combine lychees, reserved syrup and lemon juice in a blender. Blend until smooth. Strain mixture into a bowl. Add sparkling wine; stir to combine. Pour mixture into a baking dish; stir once. Freeze overnight.

2 Scrape the granita, using the back of a fork; pile into chilled martini glasses. Top with more sparkling wine and a whole lychee, if desired.

Nutrition information
Per serving: 146 calories, 0 g fat, 0 g saturated fat, 0 mg cholesterol, 22 g carbohydrates, 0 g protein, 7 mg sodium, 0 g fiber

Photo credits

John Dziekan: Pages 32, 76

Bob Fila: Pages 14, 16, 18, 28, 30, 38, 40, 64, 86, 88, 92, 94

Bill Hogan: Pages 8-9, 12, 42, 52, 56, 58, 66, 68, 70, 82, 98, 102

James F. Quinn: Page 80

Bonnie Trafelet: Pages 50, 62

Index